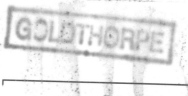

Warrior • 112

US Marine Rifleman 1939–45

Pacific Theater

Gordon L Rottman · Illustrated by Howard Gerrard

First published in Great Britain in 2006 by Osprey Publishing,
Midland House, West Way, Botley, Oxford OX2 0PH, UK
443 Park Avenue South, New York, NY 10016, USA
E-mail: info@ospreypublishing.com

© 2006 Osprey Publishing Ltd.

A CIP catalog record for this book is available from the British Library

ISBN-10: 1 84176 972 X
ISBN-13: 978 1 84176 972 1

Page layout by: Mark Holt
Typeset in Helvetica Neue and ITC New Baskerville
Index by David Worthington
Originated by EPC Direct UK Ltd, Cwmbran, UK
Printed in China through World Print Ltd.

06 07 08 09 10   10 9 8 7 6 5 4 3 2 1

FOR A CATALOG OF ALL BOOKS PUBLISHED BY OSPREY MILITARY AND
AVIATION PLEASE CONTACT:

NORTH AMERICA
Osprey Direct, c/o Random House Distribution Center, 400 Hahn Road,
Westminster, MD 21157
E-mail: info@ospreydirect.com

ALL OTHER REGIONS
Osprey Direct UK, P.O. Box 140 Wellingborough, Northants, NN8 2FA, UK
E-mail: info@ospreydirect.co.uk

www.ospreypublishing.com

Acknowledgments

The author is indebted to Ben Franks (former Chief
Historian of the Marine Corps and 6thMarDiv) and William
T. Paull (10th Marines). He is especially appreciative of
Chuck Melson and the staff at the Marine Corps Historical
Center for their assistance.

Artist's note

Readers may care to note that the original paintings from
which the color plates in this book were prepared are
available for private sale. All reproduction copyright
whatsoever is retained by the Publishers. All inquiries
should be addressed to:

Howard Gerrard
11 Oaks Road
Tenterden
Kent
TN30 6RD
UK

The Publishers regret that they can enter into no
correspondence upon this matter.

Abbreviations

IIIAC	III Amphibious Corps
VAC	V Amphibious Corps
amtrac	amphibian tractor
BAR	Browning Automatic Rifle
head	bathroom
CO	commanding officer
CP	command post
Dago	Marine Corps Training Center, Marine Corps Base, San Diego, California
DI	Drill Instructor
FMF	Fleet Marine Force
FMFPac	Fleet Marine Force Pacific
HBT	Herringbone twill
LCVP	Landing Craft, Vehicle, Personnel
LSD	Landing Ship, Dock
LST	Landing Ship, Tank
MarBde	Marine Brigade
MarDiv	Marine Division
PFC	private 1st class
PI	Marine Corps Recruit Depot, Marine Barracks, Parris Island, South Carolina
PX	Post Exchange
RCT	Regimental Combat Team
ROTC	Reserve Officers' Training Corps
Taps	the last bugle call blown at night, signaling lights out
USMC	United States Marine Corps
WP	white phosphorus

Editor's note

All uncredited images in this book are used courtesy of the
USMC.

CONTENTS

INTRODUCTION	4
CHRONOLOGY	6
CONSCRIPTION	7
TRAINING	12
APPEARANCE	19
Combat garb	
EQUIPMENT	25
Weapons	
BELIEF AND BELONGING	32
CAMP PENDLETON	41
CONDITIONS OF SERVICE	44
ON CAMPAIGN	47
Attack on Roi-Namur • Rest and recovery • Wounded in action	
THE AFTERMATH OF BATTLE	58
COLLECTIONS, MUSEUMS, AND REENACTMENT	60
BIBLIOGRAPHY	61
COLOR PLATE COMMENTARY	61
INDEX	64

US MARINE RIFLEMAN 1939–45: PACIFIC THEATER

INTRODUCTION

On December 7, 1941, the headline of the *New York Daily News* proclaimed "JAPS BOMB HAWAII" – few people at the time knew where Pearl Harbor was. Thousands of young men flocked to recruiting stations anxious to get into the fight. Many who wanted a crack at the Japanese "before the war was over" signed up with the United States Marine Corps (USMC), counting on a Corps slogan, "First to Fight," to fulfill its promise. For the men of the 1st and 2d Marine Divisions (MarDivs) this would hold true. By February 1942 the recruiting station lines had dwindled. Those who wished to get into the fight early had already enlisted. Most others, beyond enthusiastic youngsters coming of age, would wait for a letter of invitation from Uncle Sam. Two days short of the anniversary of the Pearl Harbor attack, President Franklin Roosevelt signed an order ending voluntary enlistment of draft age men. By February 1943 intake at Marine recruit depots had reduced to a trickle of 18-year-olds who had enlisted in the Marine Corps Reserve at 17, or younger if they had lied about their age (this was an era in which birth certificates were not always rendered). The Corps' age-old tradition of accepting only volunteers had ended.

Since its formation the Corps had provided ships' detachments, landing parties, expeditionary forces, and naval station guards. In 1933 the Fleet Marine Force (FMF) was established to provide a dedicated expeditionary and overseas base defense force.

The Marines were not a second land army, but a specialized amphibious force with its own service elements and air arm to support the Navy. By 1944 there were over 472,000 marines in two amphibious corps, six divisions, and a large service force. The US Army had 89 divisions, of which 21 served in the Pacific Theater. On the eve of the Pearl Harbor attack, the Corps had consisted of 65,881 officers and men. Ten days later it was authorized a strength of 104,000. There was much to do to bring the two existing divisions and the recently authorized and yet to be activated third division up to strength and achieve the necessary training.

With the mission of supporting the Navy in mind, it was originally envisioned that one Marine division would serve with the Atlantic Fleet and

A typical Marine Corps recruiting poster offered no illusions as to what marines did. Many young men were attracted to the Corps because of the promise to get into the fight first.

participate in the North Africa landings. The FMF, though, would be entirely committed to the Pacific Theater: the ultimate naval campaign. The 3d MarDiv was activated in September 1942. The need for additional Marine divisions was soon realized. Existing and new units began to assemble on the east and west coasts in early 1943, and in August 1943 the 4th MarDiv was activated. It was followed by the 5th MarDiv in January 1944 and the 6th MarDiv, organized around an existing brigade, in September.

The marines manning these units were just average American boys, mostly from low- or medium-income families. Some came from the southern states, but the states that contributed the most troops to the Corps were New York, Pennsylvania, Illinois, California, and Texas. They had spent their childhood and early adulthood under the cloud of the Great Depression. They came from farms, small towns, or big cities: their backgrounds reflected the diverse society of the country they would fight for. These young men, being raised during the Great Depression, had often led a tough life and were used to some degree of privation. Many were as tough as the Drill Instructors (DIs) who would turn them into marines. Their average age was 18 to 22. They were patriotic, dedicated, and willing to fight for the duration. They took the battle cry "Remember Pearl Harbor" seriously. To the average American, the sneak attack on Pearl Harbor was a worse transgression than all other Japanese acts of aggression combined.

A marine fills his canteen from a 36-gallon (136-liter) Lister bag. These canvas bags were slung from tree limbs or tent pole tripods to provide water in rear areas. They were fitted with six spigots and were provided with cone-shaped canvas covers to protect them from dust.

CHRONOLOGY

1939
Sep 8   US President declares "limited emergency" to strengthen national defense in response to German invasion of Poland. USMC Reserve ordered to mobilize in stages.

1940
Sep 16   Selective Training and Service Act established, authorizing conscription.

1941
Feb 1   1st and 2d Marine Brigades (MarBdes) redesignated as 1st and 2d MarDivs in Cuba and San Diego, California, respectively.
May 27   US President declares "full emergency" and authorizes armed forces to readiness levels to repel a threat to the Western hemisphere.
Jun 30   Last USMC reservists mobilized.
Dec 7   Japan attacks Pearl Harbor and the Philippines.
Dec 8–10   Japan assaults Guam; US forces surrender.
Dec 12   Japanese Army lands on Luzon.
Dec 23   Japan assaults Wake Island; US forces surrender.

1942
Apr 9   US–Filipino forces surrender Bataan.
May 5–6   Japan assaults Corregidor; US–Filipino forces surrender.
Jun 1   USMC ordered to accept African-Americans.
Jun 4–5   Battle of Midway.
Aug 7   1st MarDiv assaults Guadalcanal-Tulagi.
Sep 16   3d MarDiv activated at Camp Elliott, California.
Sep 25   Camp Joseph H. Pendleton, California established.
Dec 5   Voluntary enlistment terminated.

1943
Jun 20   New Georgia operations commence.
Jul–Aug   Units to be assigned to 4th MarDiv concentrate at Camp Pendleton.
Aug 16   4th MarDiv activated at Camp Pendleton.
Nov 1   3d MarDiv assaults Cape Torokina, Bougainville.
Nov 20   2d MarDiv assaults Tarawa Atoll.
Dec 26   1st MarDiv assaults Cape Gloucester, New Britain.

1944
Jan 6–13   4th MarDiv departs for Central Pacific.
Jan 21   5th MarDiv activated at Camp Pendleton.
Jan 31   4th MarDiv assaults Roi-Namur.
Feb 13   4th MarDiv departs for Hawaii.
Feb 21–25   4th MarDiv arrives at Maui, Hawaii.
Apr 19   1st Prov (Provisional) MarBde formed on Guadalcanal.
May 29   4th MarDiv departs for Saipan.
Jun 5   Fleet Marine Force Pacific (FMFPac) established as type command for Marine forces in the Pacific Ocean Areas.
Jun 15   V Amphibious Corps (VAC) with 2d and 4th MarDivs assaults Saipan.
Jul 21   III Amphibious Corps (IIIAC) with 3d MarDiv and 1st Prov MarBde assaults Guam.
Jul 24   VAC with 4th and 2d MarDivs assaults Tinian.
Aug 7–14   4th MarDiv departs Tinian.
Aug 18–Sep 1 4th MarDiv arrives at Maui, Hawaii.
Sep 6   1st MarDiv assaults Peleliu.
Sep 7   6th MarDiv activated on Guadalcanal.
Sep 15   1st MarDiv assaults Peleliu.

1945
Jan 27   4th MarDiv departs for Iwo Jima.

Feb 19	4th, 5th, and 3d MarDivs assault Iwo Jima.
Mar 20	4th MarDiv departs for Hawaii.
Apr 1	IIIAC 1st and 6th MarDivs assault Okinawa with Army troops.
May 7	Germany surrenders (V-E Day).
Aug 6	Atomic bomb dropped on Hiroshima.
Aug 9	Atomic bomb dropped on Nagasaki.
Aug 14	Japan announces its intention to accept unconditional surrender terms.
Aug 30	Task Force A (4th Marines) lands at Yokosuka on Tokyo Bay.
Sep 2	Japan surrenders (V-J Day).
Sep 22	2d and 5th MarDivs begin occupation of Kyushu Island, Japan.
Sep 30	1st and 6th MarDivs begin occupation of North China.
Oct 6–Nov 3	4th MarDiv elements depart for California.
Oct 12–Nov 9	Last 4th MarDiv elements arrive at Camp Pendleton.
Nov 28	4th MarDiv is deactivated.

CONSCRIPTION

President Roosevelt declared a "limited emergency" in response to the German invasion of Poland in September 1939. This permitted voluntary mobilization of Marine reservists. The Marine Corps Organized Reserve was ordered to active duty in October 1940 to be followed by the Fleet and Volunteer Reserves. The Marine Corps Reserve as an organization was terminated in order to eliminate distinctions between regulars and reservists – to form a single unified Marine Corps.

The President directed the implementation of peacetime conscription in the form of the Selective Training and Service Act in September 1940. The act provided for 12 months' service. All men between the age of 18 and 65 were to register, and those aged up to 45 were liable for induction, although the maximum authorized age of induction was 38. In late 1941 after the President declared a "full emergency," the draft period was extended to 18 months.

Prior to the war and the authorized expansion of the Marine Corps, the draft was of no concern. With the country just coming out of the

---

NOTICE OF CLASSIFICATION App. Not Req.

_____
   (First name)   (Middle name)   (Last name)

Order No. _____ has been classified in Class _____

   (Until _____, 19_____)
       (Insert date for Class II-A and II-B only)

by ☐ Local Board.
    ☐ Board of Appeal (by vote of _____ to _____).
    ☐ President.

_____, 19_____ _____
(Date of mailing)   (Member of local board)

The law requires you, subject to heavy penalty for violation, to have this notice, in addition to you're your registration Certificate (Form 2), in your personal possession at all times—to exhibit it upon request to authorized officials—to surrender it, upon entering the armed forces, to your commanding officer.
DSS Form 57. (Rev. 3-29-43)

A Notice of Classification or "draft card," which all registered men carried and turned in when conscripted.

Marines practice descending a simulated ship's side on a cargo net. Note the diamond-shaped rope pattern, making footing difficult. Most landing nets were a square pattern.

Great Depression, many young men found the Corps' pay of $21 a month appealing, even with a four-year enlistment, and hungered for travel, challenge, and adventure. Hollywood movies about the Corps enticed others. To many the Corps seemed more attractive than the Army or Navy. They volunteered before the draft caught them, or because they wanted to sign up with the best. Many did not bother to register for the draft and would find themselves receiving warning letters as they fought on South Pacific islands. Seventeen-year-olds could enlist with their parents' or guardian's permission. Some quit high school to join up, and many had not even made it that far in school before they enlisted. Some were attracted by the recruiting NCOs' blue uniforms, or the image of the "Devil Dogs" of the Great War, or the "old salt" marines serving in exotic lands during the recent Banana Wars (1898–1934). The influx of volunteers immediately after Pearl Harbor was huge. They soon exceeded the Corps' authorized strength. There were examples of entire high school football teams signing up together. The pre-Pearl Harbor volunteers, even if they had been in the Corps only a year, were the "old timers" that brought the traditions and *esprit de corps* of the "Old Corps" into the new, rapidly expanding force. With the declaration of war, service was extended to the "duration plus six months."

On December 5, 1942, voluntary enlistment in all armed services was ordered to cease. This measure provided a more efficient means of mass induction by not distracting recruiting personnel. There was a final rush to volunteer before the order took effect on January 1, 1943. However, even after the order, conscripts received by the Marine Corps were in practical terms still volunteers. Headquarters, Marine Corps detailed liaison officers to state draft boards, and NCOs to Armed Forces Induction Centers to coordinate the assignment of draftees preferring the Corps. If current Corps quotas did not provide a billet for called-up individuals, the draft boards often deferred the applicants until such openings were authorized. In this way the Corps received 224,000 inductees, whom the Corps called Selective Service Volunteers (SS-V) or, less formally, "draftee-volunteers" or "hand-cuffed volunteers." From the beginning of 1943, recruiters could also sign up 17-year-olds in the Marine Corps Reserve. Some 60,000 enlisted, and on turning 18 they reported for active duty. The four regional Recruiting Divisions were redesignated Procurement Divisions in May 1943, overseeing the draftee-volunteers, recruiting 17-year-olds, and procuring officers. Each division had six or seven recruiting stations co-located with Navy recruiting stations in major cities. Men classified 4-F (unfit for service) lived with a sense of shame, and there were even occasional suicides.

The draft was conducted by a national lottery system. After draft registration numbers were assigned, a draw was held on October 29, 1940. A total of 365 dated capsules were drawn in random order and the dates announced in newspapers. Each date was assigned a number from 1–365 in the order drawn. The 1-As (available for military service) were called in the order their birth date was drawn: most inductees and volunteers were born between 1919 and 1926. This was repeated each year with the age bracket extended until the draft was canceled in 1947. When their number was drawn, the men received an eight-page questionnaire, used to determine their eligibility for military service.

There was a complex system of deferments and exemptions based on physical qualifications, religious grounds, and essential employment, which included those involved in defense industries and farm workers. Draft exemptions were determined by local draft boards; there was usually one board per county, or several in large cities. There were no education exemptions, although college students undertaking Reserve Officers' Training Corps (ROTC) or other officer training programs were deferred. Nor were there exemptions for family hardships such as caring for ill or elderly parents. Inducted conscientious objectors were mostly assigned to medical services.

If selected, a draftee received an Order to Report for Induction and would report to his local draft board. This fateful letter could have been received as few as ten days before the reporting date. At this point it was not certain whether he would actually be inducted. From the draft board office he would be taken by bus or train to the nearest Armed Forces Induction Center, usually at a major city Post Office, federal building, National Guard armory, or local military base, for a simple physical examination and some administrative paperwork. Those who were selected were assembled and, if they desired, were allowed home for a week to put their affairs in order. Most accepted this option, but could be sent straight on to the reception center if they so requested. The others would return the next week and take part in a mass swearing-in alongside men going into other services.

Selective Service classifications	
1-A	Available for military service
1-A-O	Conscientious objector, available for non-combatant service
1-B	Available for limited military service
1-B-C	Conscientious objector, available for non-combatant limited service
1-C	Land or naval forces coast guard
1-H	28 years of age prior to July 1, 1941, and not inducted by that date
2-A	Necessary man in his civilian category
2-B	Necessary man in national defense
3-A	Man with dependents
4-A	Man who has completed service
4-B	Official deferred by law
4-D	Minister of divinity student
4-E	Conscientious objector fit for service, available for work of national importance
4-E-ES	Conscientious objector fit for limited service
4-H	Conscientious objector over 28 years of age prior to July 1, 1941
4-F	Morally, mentally, or physically unfit

A Marine officer swears in young recruits at an Armed Forces Induction Center. Marine recruiting NCOs wearing dress blues stand at the rear of the formation. The American and Marine Corps colors flank the ceremony.

ORDER TO REPORT FOR INDUCTION
GREETING:
Having submitted yourself to a Local Board composed of your neighbors for the purpose of determining your availability for training and service in the armed forces of the United States, you are hereby notified that you have now been selected for training and service in the

_____.
(Army, Navy, Marine Corps)
You will, therefore, report to the Local Board named above at _____
(Place of reporting)
at _____m., on the _____ day of _____, 19___.
(Hour of reporting)

The inductee would say his goodbyes after a farewell family dinner, and report again to the induction station. Transportation costs were paid. The young man's volunteering or induction was often announced in the local newspaper. Families with sons in the military displayed a Blue Star Service Banner in their windows, a small rectangular banner with a blue star for each serving son. If a son was lost a gold star was displayed.

Marine recruits were transferred to one of two places by bus or train. If they lived east of the Mississippi River they went to Marine Corps Recruit Depot, Marine Barracks, Parris Island, South Carolina, or if to the west, to Marine Corps Training Center, Marine Corps Base, San Diego, California. They had a change of clothes, a toilet kit, perhaps a few dollars, some meal tickets provided by the induction center, and a sense of apprehension.

There has been a great deal of debate over the differences between the two recruit training centers, an argument that still continues today. The Commandant of the Marine Corps permitted both to develop their own curricula. There were differences in the hours allotted to subjects, with more or less emphasis in certain areas, and a few minor techniques were taught differently. One officer commented that the only real difference was that San Diego ("Dago") taught marines to jump from a sinking ship with both hands protecting the face, and Parris Island ("PI") to use one hand for face protection and the other to protect the crotch. There were other differences, of course, but the variance in instruction made less difference than the environment. PI was in a remote area, essentially a big sandbar mostly surrounded by swamps. It was hot and humid, infested with sand fleas, flies, and mosquitoes in the summer, but enduring a cold winter and Atlantic storms. It was 55 miles (88.5km) southwest of Charleston, with the small town of Beaufort 5 miles (8km) distant for the rare liberty. Dago, on the other hand, was in sub-tropical southern California with a year-round pleasant climate. San Diego was immediately outside the gate. Marines training there and at camps Elliott and Pendleton were called "Hollywood marines," even though Los Angeles was a considerable distance away. There was a degree of competition and resentment between PI and Hollywood marines.

Many of the marines who found themselves on the bus to PI or Dago were away from home for the first time, with few having ever been farther from their birthplace than the neighboring county. They were from major urban, suburban, and rural areas, and small towns. Many accents sounded strange to them and the sights they saw were equally as strange as they traveled westwards.

To modern eyes the Corps was bigoted. It strongly resisted the enlistment of African-Americans and women, and was the last service to accept either. "Colored troops," as African-Americans were then officially designated, were kept completely segregated and were seldom seen by most marines. Hispanics were integrated into the Corps, but were few in number. Fewer still were Native-Americans – most Marines were not aware of the Navajo Code-Talkers. Sometimes ethnic minorities were singled out for harassment. Men with noticeable physical differences were also often picked on. Those with a college education, or who appeared to come from families of means seemed to be

The 8×14-in. (20×35.5cm) Blue Star Service Banner (red border, white center, blue star, gold fringe and cord) as displayed in the windows of homes with a family member in the military; one star for each service member. If a serviceman was killed the blue star was replaced by one of gold. (Military/Tactical & Outdoor)

Camp Elliott, California, with its H-shaped barracks and administrative buildings still under construction. To the right are the tent encampments ("tent city"). Camp Elliott was where west coast infantrymen were trained, along with tankers.

particularly targeted for harassment by DIs. Eighty percent of a platoon would be teenagers, but there were a few over the age of 20. They generally proved to be the platoon's unofficial internal leaders, keeping the youngsters in line when they cut-up or "grab-assed" (caused mischief or perpetrated pranks) too much when DIs were not present.

TRAINING

In the spring of 1943 a new batch of recruits rolled into Marine Corps Recruit Depot (MCRD), at the San Diego Training Center, to be astounded by the palm-lined entrance road and Spanish-style architecture. The first few days were a blur. They were turned off the bus by a sergeant, herded into a formation by lining their toes up on a white stripe, and told to ground their bags on their right side. The introduction to discipline was immediate. The recruits or "Boots" (there were worse names) learned quickly never to smile, to look straight ahead, to speak only when spoken to, to answer "Yes, Sir" or "No, Sir." There were no excuses for mistakes or infractions, and they had to pay very close attention to what was being said. "Boots" were already being dropped for 25 push-ups for the slightest transgression. Names were checked off, the recruits were broken down into squads, and then marched into a large two-story stucco barracks. Double-stacked bunks or "racks" lined both walls and an end-to-end double row of bunks stretched down the center, leaving two aisles. Next to each pair of bunks were two olive-drab plywood locker boxes and two 3-gallon (11.4-liter) galvanized buckets. The men were given the opportunity to turn in any contraband items, no questions asked (weapons, knives, straight razors, liquor, obscene materials).

With buckets in hand, they followed the sergeant single file to the Post Exchange (PX) – "ge-dunk shop." They were told what to place in their buckets: scrubbing and shoe brushes, bath soap, box of laundry powder, toothbrush, toothpaste, safety razor and blades, bag of Bull Durham® tobacco, Zigzag® cigarette papers (they would roll their own, no "ready-mades"), brown boot polish, Brasso® polish, two white bath towels embossed "U.S. MARINE CORPS" on a red strip, and other necessities.

They also bought a copy of *The Marine's Handbook* ("Red Book") for $1. After learning that $15 would be deducted from their $50 a month pay for these PX purchases, they were led to the barber shop. Seated in the chairs, they were asked if they would like a trim around the ears while their scalps were sheared bare.

The recruits' next visit was to the quartermaster. Entering the warehouse-like building, they were confronted with shelf after shelf of uniforms and equipment. Ordered to strip, they were given a cardboard box on which they wrote their addresses and put their "civvies" in to be sent home. They were issued with green dungarees, a utility cap,

Recruits stand in formation after unloading from the train as a local boy looks on. Here NCOs from the recruit depot will pick them up, bussing them into a very different world.

white underwear, and white socks. The quartermasters issuing the uniforms merely "eyeballed" their clothing sizes. Care was taken, though, for the fitting of leather service shoes or "boondockers." Carrying buckets in their right hands, clothing in the left, and their two pairs of boondockers hanging around their necks, the recruits returned to barracks. They were given padlocks for the locker boxes and drew bedding: two sheets, two wool blankets, and a pillow case. A key was placed on their "dog tag" chain – the tags could never be removed, even to unlock a locker, a task requiring the recruit to get down on all fours to do so. A second key was retained by the sergeant with the man's name on a tag. The men spent the rest of the day learning how to make bunks, stow gear, and the dos and don'ts of barracks life. They could not sit or lay on their bunks until "lights out," when an instructor entered the squad bay. The first to see him would shout "Attention" and they would all remain in that position until told "As you were" or "At ease." The recruits could only smoke when told the "smoking lamp is lit" and cigarettes were extinguished when the "smoking lamp is out." They could not leave the barracks unless told. The squad bay and head (bathroom) were to be kept spotless at all times. They also learned what it meant to be part of the naval services. The floor was the "deck," the walls "bulkheads," the ceiling the "overhead," stairs were "ladders," etc.

Over the next couple of days the recruits completed more paperwork and signed up for National Service Life Insurance at $6.40 a month for a $10,000 payout, a benefit the service had provided since October 1940. They received a complete physical, dental examination, and seemingly endless inoculations. They also took a simple mental skills test, and, unknown to them, their paperwork was being examined by classification specialists to determine their fate. Their actual assignment, though, would have more to do with the needs of the service at the given moment, rather than any particular qualifications or skills they might possess.

The issue of uniforms was the first step towards becoming a marine. Here recruits are issued forest-green and khaki service uniforms. The marine wearing the sun helmet is not a Drill Instructor, but an NCO guiding the recruits through their first days until assigned to a recruit platoon.

Mass uniform and equipment issue. Recruits freshly shorn of their hair pack their basic issue into sea bags.

Many of the recruits had assumed they would spend boot camp in the barracks, but one morning they were ordered to fall out with everything, including bedding, packed in their canvas sea bags and lockers. They lugged the impossible loads across the broad, blistering drill field to rows of green-painted steel Quonset huts. Platoons of recruits on the drill field shouted a disparaging, "You'll be sorreeee!" One of the new groups of 60 men in ill-fitting dungarees found themselves facing a tough-looking sergeant and two plain, mean-looking corporals wearing starched khaki uniforms and dark olive-drab field or "campaign" hats – these men were their DIs. They quickly learned that Sergeant "Sandbag" and corporals "Tightlips" and "Barbedwire" held absolute authority of life and death over them. The DIs informed the recruits that they were an insult to the Corps and all the real marines who had gone before them, and were no doubt here because their god-fearing families had thrown them out in embarrassment. They were now members of a numbered recruit platoon[1] organized into three 20-man squads. After a period of screaming, yelling, and being dropped for push-ups, the platoon was herded into the two 20×48ft (6.1×14.6m) Quonset huts assigned to them. The head and showers were in a separate building. The men made their bunks and stowed their gear, with the corporals all the time shouting that they were too slow. Seemingly they could do nothing right; they were too slow, too sloppy, and plain dumb. Over the coming miserable days a desire grew to please the DIs no matter what, not to halt the harassment (they knew that would never end) but to prove they had what it took to be marines. They pushed themselves. A small number were washed out.

The DIs are a Marine Corps institution and they are the means by which young men are turned into marines. Prior to the war there was more time available to train and indoctrinate recruits – up to ten weeks. DIs coached and, in effect, mentored recruits. They were hand-picked and used a fair, but firm methodology. There was harassment, but it was meted out in doses and only when necessary. At the time there was only a small number of recruits, and they were motivated by more professional considerations of duty; they were not driven by a war of preservation. In the early 1940s, however, with an unprecedented influx of thousands of green young men pouring into the Corps, a means had to be found to hammer them into battle-ready marines; and hammer was the right word. The Corps' training mechanism could barely handle the load. Even training areas, ranges, quarters, support facilities, and equipment were in short supply. Recruits could not be "nurtured" into marines. It had to be done fast and effectively. DIs were no longer hand-picked, but selected for their gruff appearance, loud voices, and lack of concern over

1 Recruit platoons were numbered in sequence through the war at San Diego and Parris Island. Though assigned to a lettered training company as part of one of seven recruit battalions at Dago, recruits only identified with their platoon.

hurting feelings. They were relentless disciplinarians. Many had only been in the Corps for a limited time; some DI corporals had only just graduated from boot camp. In the early days few had combat experience. The old salts, the career marines with Banana Wars experience, fleet marines, and "Old China" hands were needed in the combat units to train and lead the first marines into combat. It would not be until mid-1943, when veterans from the South Pacific were rotated back to the States, that vets began to be assigned as DIs in any numbers. The early, less-experienced DIs were often unsure of themselves, having little practical experience leading men, and they relied on their position of authority to bully recruits and to make up for their own lack of confidence. There were abuses and humiliation, which were often ignored; the job at hand was too critical to allow concern about niceties and there was little time in which to accomplish the job. Boot camp had been cut back to three weeks before the war to accommodate the build-up; insufficient time to train and condition a recruit to any acceptable level – they were only given a week's rifle and marksmanship training. Boot was lengthened to seven weeks by the end of 1940 and eight in 1944.

Here marines descend a landing net, from a high wharf constructed to simulate a ship, into a Landing Craft, Personnel (Large).

The new recruits spent the evening scrubbing down their quarters until lights out was ordered and Taps sounded over the base loudspeaker at 2200hrs. There were seven or eight double bunks on each side of the squad room. The rifle racks were at the back wall and there were two 30-gallon (114-liter) galvanized garbage cans in the center aisle, which were cleaned with brass polish. The DIs had their own rooms in the huts and nothing escaped them. Men were assigned two-hour fire-watch shifts through the night, ensuring that no one smoked, and guarding the racked rifles. They would holystone (soft sandstone block) the deck once a day. Each evening they would wash a set of dungarees, skivvies, and socks.

The lights came on at 0400hrs with DIs screaming for the men to fall out of their racks, amid buckets being kicked across the deck: "Hit the deck!" The dreary-eyed platoon had 30 minutes to wash before falling out in formation. They had to shave even if a razor had never before touched their faces. Roll was called by the glare of a flashlight and they marched to the chow hall. The men sat down on benches at plank tables when ordered, and other recruits, obviously "senior" as they were sun-tanned and fuzz was growing back on their heads,[2] served them platters of eggs, bacon, and pancakes and pitchers of coffee, milk, and orange juice. They were not to speak unless asking for food to be passed. They were told "take all you want, but eat all you take." Most began to gain weight, not just from the food, but also from exercise. They ate a lot of chicken, pork chops, and ground beef, had plenty of potatoes in all forms, and lots of vegetables and fresh breads. On Sunday there was

2 These recruits had completed their week of range firing and would pull a week of mess duty.

always chicken and on Monday chicken leftovers. There was fish on Friday even though the "Mackerel-snappers" – Catholics – were given wartime dispensation to eat meat. Likewise, Jews were allowed to eat non-Kosher foods. It was a seven-day week, although Sundays were dedicated to church call, administrative requirements, and cleaning quarters, gear and uniforms.

In formation in front of their huts they were told that here was a landmark day: they would be issued with their rifles. At the armory they received a .30-cal. M1903 Springfield rifle and a long bayonet. They had to memorize the rifle's serial number by the time they returned to barracks, and there they learned the difference between a rifle and a gun. The first recruit making this error in nomenclature demonstrated the difference by holding each piece of equipment in opposite hands reciting, "This is my rifle, this is my gun. This is for fighting, this is for fun." The day was spent learning to disassemble and assemble the rifle and how to meticulously clean it. They were told they would have to disassemble and assemble it blindfolded, that they must be able to correctly name every single part, and that the rifle would become their best friend. To drop or otherwise mistreat a rifle was a cardinal sin.

The first four weeks were spent at the depot undertaking a great deal of close-order drill, manual of arms, physical fitness drills, bayonet training, obstacle courses, lectures on field sanitation, military courtesies (when and whom to salute), recognizing rank, military law (Articles of the Government of the Navy – "Rocks and Shoals"), and guard duty. Field training was conducted in the form of forced marches, first aid, signaling, gas warfare, cover and concealment, scouting and patrolling. They were taken to the nearby Del Mar Race Track, closed for the duration of the war and now called Camp C.J. Miller, where they were taught combat swimming and water survival. Harassment continued relentlessly. The DIs' goal was to break these young men down to the lowest level and then gradually build up their confidence and self-esteem. They had to work as a team and put aside individual concerns and comforts. The recruits, even though they had to work together, had little time to talk to one another and discover personal details.

Recruits during their two weeks at the rifle range march in formation with the M1903 rifle. Their rifle scorecards are pinned behind the globe and anchor on their sun helmets.

Barrack and full equipment layout inspections were held on Saturdays. The early inspections were disasters. DIs raked meticulously displayed gear off bunks with a sweep of the arm and threw locker boxes down the aisles, scattering the contents. The DIs seemed to introduce them to new punishments daily: one DI telling them to dig a 6ft-cubed (1.8m-cubed) hole and another DI telling them to fill it in; running around the drill field or on the spot with the rifle at high port (held at arm's length over the head); holding two partly filled buckets of water in outstretched arms; and ice-cold showers. Some punishments were reserved for specific infractions. Failure to shave resulted in a "dry shave" without lather or water. If the DI wished to make a deeper impression he had another recruit do the shaving. A recruit found with his hand in his pockets had the pockets filled with sand and sewn shut. A "Boot" who could not seem to do things correctly would stand to attention in front of his hut clad in "skivvies" with a bucket over his head shouting, "I am the platoon screw-up" to all passing by. Passing DIs would rap their swagger sticks on the bucket. A man continually causing problems, one who could not get it right, brought grief on the entire platoon. DIs were not beyond group punishment to make the point that they were all in this together. A "blanket party" might be called for, a late-night visit by the nonconformist's platoon mates. A blanket would be thrown over the transgressor and he was held down as others applied fists. Even with the draft the Marines considered themselves a volunteer service. Men could gripe, but only to a point. They would be reminded that they asked for this, they volunteered. In the eyes of the Corps the fact that they were volunteers meant they could be driven harder and more could be expected of them.

For the fifth and sixth weeks the company moved to Camp Calvin B. Matthews, 13 miles (20km) north of San Diego. They lived in squad tents with wooden decks, a "tent city." Here they focused totally on rifle marksmanship, conducting known-distance (KD) range firing. This was extremely important, as all marines were considered as riflemen first, regardless of specialty. Harassment here was reduced to allow them to concentrate on qualifying as Marksmen, Sharpshooters, or Expert Riflemen, and they would *all* qualify. As motivation to fire Expert, they would receive $5 extra a month. They also fired the .45-cal. M1911A1 Colt pistol for familiarization. Most marines have fond memories of this period.

Upon their return to Dago the recruits pulled a week of mess duty and post work details. Yet again they had not seen the PX, had any "poggy bait" (candy), soda, or beer, and liberty was beyond hope. The DIs, however, were starting to treat them somewhat like humans, even joked with them sometimes; they were feeling like they might become marines. They conducted their first parade in forest-green service uniforms. It was their first time seeing officers. They were given a speech about what they had achieved and the service they would soon provide the country, and they were also given their globe and anchor insignia. They were now marines because the DIs actually told them so, and even drank a brew with them. This is when the platoon photograph was taken, with the new marines in their service uniforms and sun helmets, gripping their rifles in their hands, and standing on a five-tier bleacher with their DI front row center, behind the sign bearing their platoon number and the year.

The recruits were quite proud of themselves at this point. They were in the best physical condition of their lives, they were sun-tanned, had put on weight, and had a great deal of self-confidence. Through it all the enemy was seldom spoken of. There were no propaganda speeches or political exhortations other than the occasional Hollywood movie, which offered more in the way of propaganda than any government effort.

Much to their surprise, the recruits were given a week's leave and they headed home wearing their unadorned khakis via bus and train. This was new to the Corps, as leave after boot camp had only begun to be granted in the spring of 1943; previously they had gone directly to specialty training, then were assigned to a unit and deployed, often without any leave. They all returned at the appointed time, by midnight. They had been sternly lectured about what would happen if they failed to return on time – they were not told they had a 24-hour grace period to return from leave and were dismayed when one man came in a day late and nothing was said. He had been informed of the grace period by an older brother. If an individual failed to report in from leave or liberty at the required time, he was declared Absent Without Leave (AWOL) and was subject to disciplinary action. If he had still not reported in after 30 days, he became a deserter, subject to arrest by the police and sought after by the FBI.

Water survival training included basic swimming (enough to stay afloat and to swim away from a sinking ship), abandoning a ship by jumping, and assisting a wounded man. Here recruits have removed their trousers, tied off the legs, and inflated them.

It was after leave that the men learned their future assignments, which had been much anticipated. The Marine Corps had 21 occupation fields, each with numerous individual specialties. Some men found themselves going to Camp Pendleton, 32 miles (51km) north of Dago, for artillery, scout and sniper, engineer, amphibian tractor, or signal training. Most, though, were assigned to the Infantry Training Battalion at Camp Elliott, 12 miles (19km) northeast of Dago.

Camp Elliott covered 32,000 acres (12,928 hectares) on Kearney Mesa, a dry area of scrub brush, rolling hills, and ravines. The infantry students were housed in two-story H-shaped wooden barracks with squad bays in the arms of the "H" and heads in the crossbar. The training was straightforward and practical, and no time was wasted on harassment. The instructors, mostly combat vets, were there only to teach them their trade. They usually had evenings off, plus weekend liberty. The three weeks' training qualified each young man as a Rifleman, Specification Code No.745. He was issued an M1 rifle and would carry it to his next assignment. He conducted more rifle firing integrated into tactical live-fire exercises, and received introduction to squad and platoon tactics, scouting and patrolling, hand and rifle grenades, basic judo and knife fighting, and familiarization firing with all battalion weapons. Other men were trained on the Browning Automatic Rifle (BAR; never pronounced "bar"), light and heavy machine guns, 60mm and 81mm mortars, or 37mm antitank gun. They were given first and second choices in which weapon they wanted to train on.

APPEARANCE

The image an observer would first note was the youth of these marines. They were kids – when the war started in 1939 they were in junior high or had just entered high school. They were lean because of the Depression years and the lack of "fast foods." Their average height was 5ft 6in. (1.67m) – the average today is 5ft 8in. (1.72m) and average weight has increased. They were proud of their Spartan uniforms and went to the expense of having them tailor fitted. There was not much on their uniforms – no shoulder insignia, name tags, or ribbons. They wore only a silver Marksman, Sharpshooter, or Expert Rifleman badge on the left breast pocket flap, bronze globe and anchor or "bird on a ball" insignia on their collars, and another on the left side of the garrison cap.[3] If qualifying on other weapons, the marine would wear a Basic Weapons Qualification Badge with bars signifying the weapons and level of qualification. Once assigned to a division they would receive a "battle blaze" for their left shoulder. A private 1st class (PFC) wore a point-up chevron on both upper sleeves – red on forest green on the winter service uniform and forest green on khaki on the summer shirt. Even old salts bore few adornments: more chevrons and diagonal hash marks on the coat's left cuff, one for each four-year hitch. Ribbons were few in number, even for prewar and South Pacific veterans.

The most distinctive Marine uniform was the "blues," the uniform that attracted many young men to the Corps. It was a uniform that most would never wear, as its general issue ceased in early 1942. From that point they were issued only to Marine Barracks, Washington; Marine Detachment, London; Marine Band, and recruiters. Individuals could purchase them, but few could afford blues.

While one recruit platoon runs the bayonet course in the background, another awaits its turn, receiving instruction on the operation and throwing of hand grenades. Every minute of time was spent in training.

---

3 Recruits were not issued with globe and anchor insignia until they graduated from boot.

RIGHT **Marine dress blues worn by a 1st sergeant, sporting two service stripes ("hash marks,"each for four years' service) and the NCO's 30-in. (76cm) sword, used in the Corps since 1875. Arguably one of the most appealing uniforms in US service, it attracted many men to the Corps, but few would actually wear it.**

FAR RIGHT **The wool forest-green winter service uniform, here worn on guard duty with rifle, cartridge belt, haversack, bayonet, and leggings.**

The forest-green winter service uniform, or "greens," was the formal uniform issued to most marines. No doubt recruits were disappointed to find they would have no blues in their sea bag, but greens were an attractive uniform. The forest green was more appealing to the eye than brownish olive-drab. The kersey wool coat or blouse had epaulettes, Marine-style (Polish-style) cuffs, pleated breast pockets, and large box-style pockets on the skirts. The buttons were dark bronze adorned with the globe and anchor insignia. A 2-in. (5cm) wide cordovan belt with an open brass buckle was worn with the coat, and was known as the "fair-weather belt." In 1943 a cloth belt with a dark bronze buckle replaced the leather item. A tan wool shirt was worn with the greens in winter. In the summer a khaki cotton shirt could be worn with the forest-green trousers without the coat. Much to the marines' chagrin the trousers had only front pockets and no hip pockets (which only officers' trousers boasted). A tan field scarf (necktie) was worn with both shirts. A 3-in. (7.6cm) long "battle pin" held the collars and scarf in place. Garrison or overseas caps were provided in forest-green wool and khaki cotton for wear with the appropriate uniform. Caps were referred to as "covers," and prior to the issue of the utility cap they were worn in the field. Ankle-high, rough-side-in cordovan service shoes were worn with greens and khakis. These dark-brown shoes were to be highly "spit-shined."

The utility uniform – "utilities" or "dungarees" – was the uniform that marines spent the most time in. The two-piece dungarees were made of cotton herringbone twill (HBT) in sage green (grayish green). The hardwearing fabric proved to be effective camouflage in the jungle. It was in this uniform that the Marines stormed Guadalcanal; previously they had worn khakis in combat. The coat (shirt) had three flapless pockets on the skirts and left breast. On the breast pocket was stenciled a black globe and anchor over which was written "USMC." Rank insignia were sometimes stenciled or crudely hand-painted in black on the upper sleeves. The front opening was secured by four black metal buttons. The trousers were unusual in that they had both front and hip pockets. The utility cap began to be issued in early 1943. It was inspired by a railroad worker's cap, had a short bill, pleats around the crown, and usually a black globe and anchor stenciled on the front. The tan web trousers belt was 1¼in. (3.2cm) wide with a brass buckle and tip, both blackened. This was worn on dungarees, khakis, and greens. Since recruits were issued two belts, they would rub off the blacking on their belt's buckle and tip, which they would Brasso® to a shine. This belt would be worn with khakis and greens. Marines became quite familiar with the sharp odor of Brasso®, a canned liquid metal polish applied with a rag and rubbed briskly. Marines would also purchase a Blitz Cloth®, a square of soft cloth impregnated with brass polish. Jeweler's paste was used to polish bronze devices.

The tan fiber tropical helmet was worn by recruits during much of their training, especially on the rifle range. A large bronze globe and anchor insignia was fitted on the front. Often, the recruits did not receive the M1 steel helmet and resin-impregnated duck liner until infantry training. For field duty recruits wore tan canvas leggings and rough-side-out dark-tan leather-laced ankle boots with non-slip composite rubber soles.

Undershirts, under drawers, and socks were white. These were often dyed in some shade of green by marines using Rit® powdered dye. In combat coffee grounds were used to dye skivvies tan or light brown. Late in the war the marines were issued with green underwear and tan socks.

All items of clothing were marked in specified locations with the owner's first and middle initials and last name in ¼-in. (6.5mm) block letters. This was done with a Carter's® permanent marking outfit with rubber letters that could be set in wooden stamp blocks.

Each marine was issued two 1¼×1½-in. (3.2×3.8cm) oval dog tags to be worn around his neck. There was a hole in both ends of the monel alloy, brass, or stainless steel tag. The second tag was attached by a short loop to the lower hole of the first. Prior to 1942 only one tag was issued with an acid-etched right index fingerprint on the back. Five lines of data were stamped on the tags: 1) surname (family name); 2) given name and middle initial (sometimes first and middle initials); 3) six-digit service number[6] and religious preference (C – Catholic, H – Hebrew [Jew], P – Protestant, or blank); 4) Tetanus inoculation date (T. or TET-month/year; e.g. T.4/43) and blood type (TYPE A, B, AB, O); and 5)

Recruit Clothing Allowance, Summer[4]	
Bag, clothing (sea bag)	1
Belt, trousers, woven	2
Belt, service	1
Blanket, wool, green	2
Cap, garrison, service, summer	2
Cap, garrison, service, winter	1
Cap, utility	1
Helmet, fiber	1
Coat, rain	1
Coat, service, winter	1
Coat, utility (dungaree shirt)	2
Drawers, cotton	6
Leggings, canvas	1 pair
Ornament, cap and hat[5]	1
Ornament, collar[5]	1 pair
Overcoat	1
Scarf, cotton (necktie)	1
Shirt, cotton	3
Shoes, field	2 pairs
Socks, cotton	6 pairs
Trousers, service, summer	2
Trousers, service, winter	1
Trousers, utility	2
Undershirts, cotton	6

---

4 Recruits at PI in the winter received a third wool blanket and lined leather gloves. After boot camp, marines were each authorized one additional pair of summer service trousers, an additional scarf and cotton shirt, and a pair of leather shoes. They could purchase further clothing items at their own expense from Quartermaster Sales.

5 The Marine Corps bronze globe and anchor insignia.

6 Officers substituted their rank prior to October 1943; later replaced by letter "O" and five-digit serial number.

A recruit traverses a three-rope bridge. Khaki garrison caps were often worn in training with the dungarees. In 1944 recruits began receiving M1 rifles rather than the M1903.

Marine Corps serial number blocks	
100000–600000	Regular volunteers
500000	17-year-old volunteers
700000	Woman Marines
800000	Reserves on active duty and volunteer inductees
900000	Inductees

USMC or USMCR. If the marine was killed, one tag would remain with the body and the other be turned in to the company command post (CP) to be forwarded to Division of Personnel (Personnel Department from July 1944).

The Marine Corps utilized a complex system of enlisted ranks with numerous specialty ranks in each of the seven pay grades. The basic ranks were private, private 1st class, corporal, sergeant, platoon sergeant, gunnery sergeant ("gunny"), and master gunnery sergeant. Pay grades 1–5 were non-commissioned officers – "noncoms." Corporal and sergeant ranks were "line NCOs," holding leadership positions and identifiable by arches ("rockers") beneath their chevrons. The others were "staff NCOs" with a bar rather than a rocker beneath their chevrons or identifiable by some other device. Originally a 1st sergeant, the senior NCO in a company or battery, could be graded 1–3, but on February 10, 1943, the 1st sergeant became grade 1 only. The 1st sergeant's diamond, which had been used between 1857 and 1937, was restored to the Corps on February 8, 1944.

Combat garb

The marine in combat was stripped down to the bare essentials. Packs were often left in the company rear to be brought up at night. In the rugged jungle terrain and across broken ground, speed and agility were essential. The marine wore faded dungarees bearing only the black

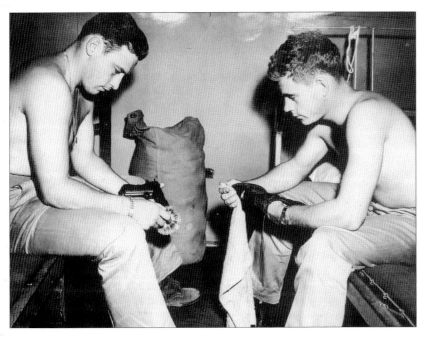

"Spit and polish," the endless task of maintaining uniforms, equipment, and weapons, is practiced in the barracks. The "T" bar at the end of the right bunk is for a mosquito net.

Enlisted Ranks, after February 10, 1943

Rank	Abbreviation	Pay Grade
Field music	FM	7
Private	Pvt	7
Field music 1st class	FM1cl	6
Assistant cook	ACk	6
Private 1st class	PFC	6
Mess corporal	MessCorp	5
Field music corporal	FMCorp	5
Field cook	FldCk	5
Corporal	Corp	5
Field music sergeant	FMSgt	4
Mess sergeant	MessSgt	4
Chief cook	CCk	4
Sergeant	Sgt	4
Staff sergeant	SSgt	3
Platoon sergeant	PlSgt	3
Technical sergeant	TSgt	2
Drum major	DrmMaj	2
Supply sergeant	SupSgt	2
Gunnery sergeant	GySgt	2
Master technical sergeant	MTSgt	1
Quartermaster sergeant	QMSgt	1
Paymaster sergeant	PMSgt	1
Master gunnery sergeant	MGySgt	1
First sergeant	1stSgt	1
Sergeant major	SgtMaj	1

globe and anchor and no rank insignia. Officers often removed their pin-on collar rank because of snipers. The utility cap was often worn under the olive-drab-painted steel helmet. A photo of his wife or girlfriend might be tucked into the helmet webbing. Reversible helmet camouflage covers began to be issued in late 1942. The more commonly used "green-side" was dark green, light olive-drab, and dark and light browns on a pale green backing, while the "brown-side" was dark and light browns, and tan on a sand backing. These same colors were used in other camouflage clothing and equipment. In monochrome photos the "brown-side" appears much lighter than the "green-side." The camo cover became a distinction of the Corps, as the Army used bare helmets or camouflage nets. The shirt was always worn outside the trousers. The marine discarded the leggings, as they chafed, restricted circulation, were too hot, and retained water after wading ashore or through swamps and streams. His trousers were unbloused and perhaps rolled up to his ankles. His boondockers were scuffed and scarred, but broken into a comfortable fit. He may have discarded his skivvies altogether, or at least the drawers. They held sweat and did not dry out, causing rashes – "jungle rot." His only gear was a cartridge belt, perhaps with suspenders (not always issued), one or two canteens, a first aid pouch, often a jungle first aid kit, a KA-Bar fighting knife, and a couple of grenades.

A typical field uniform: dungarees with helmet, M1 rifle with M1 bayonet, cartridge belt with canteen and first aid pouch, and haversack. Here the leggings are worn unbloused, but they might be worn with the trousers bloused (tucked into leggings), or discarded.

A marine's physical appearance in prolonged combat was near appalling. Weight loss was a given. He was unshaved for days or weeks, his hair grew mangy; the opportunity to bath did not exist. While sun-tanned, those fighting in dense jungle were frequently pale or their skin took on a yellow-cast owing to the tiny, bitter bright yellow atabrine anti-malaria tablets. His eyes may have appeared yellow due to jaundice. Small cuts and abrasions might develop into tropical ulcers and coral cuts could become infected. He was dehydrated, making him susceptible to shock, and took salt tablets because of excessive sweating.

EQUIPMENT

The marines used a combination of Marine and Army individual equipment. The latter came into increasing use late in the war as Army and Marine units conducted frequent joint operations. Army web gear was mostly khaki, with olive-drab gear being introduced in 1943. Marine web gear was tan, a darker shade than Army khaki. It was seldom marked with "U.S." in a high-visibility location as Army gear, but with "U.S.M.C." under flaps or on the back. Collectively, marines called their web equipment "782 gear," after the quartermaster form on which they signed for it. When a marine received his gear it was a bewildering pile of belts, straps, bags, and containers. The DIs had the platoon form up at double-arm intervals and dump their gear out of their sea bags. One of the corporals would hold up an item and the sergeant would bellow out its nomenclature. Then they talked the men through assembling and fitting it. It would require a couple of forced marches before it was adjusted to some degree of comfort. Once fully loaded with ammunition, rations, and other gear it would all have to be readjusted and rebalanced.

The M1941 pack system was the basis for load carrying. It consisted of two packs: an upper haversack with integral shoulder straps and a lower knapsack, which could be secured beneath the haversack. A full prescribed haversack load held a set of underwear, socks, poncho, rations, mess kit, knife, fork and spoon, towel, and "ditty bag" (toilet kit). A bayonet and entrenching tool were attached to the haversack. The knapsack held a set of dungarees, another set of underwear, socks, and spare shoes. A third component was the bedroll, consisting of a shelter-half ("pup tent"), three-section tent pole, five wooden tent stakes, tent guy line, mosquito net, and blanket. The M1941 pack could be configured in five assemblies:

Light marching pack – haversack without cartridge belt
Marching pack – haversack, cartridge belt, entrenching tool
Field marching pack – marching pack with bedroll
Transport pack – haversack, cartridge belt, knapsack
Field transport pack – transport pack with bedroll

What pack configuration to carry on a given training day was spelled out on the training schedule, along with the uniform of the day. Other 782 gear included an M1912 first aid pouch with a field dressing and sulfa powder or tablets, M1941 suspenders, 1-quart (roughly 1-liter) steel canteen with a metal or black plastic cap, a canteen cup with a folding handle (carried nested on the bottom of the canteen), canteen carrier, M1928 ten-pocket cartridge belt with each pocket holding two five-round M1903 rifle stripper clips or an eight-round M1 rifle clip, and a non-folding M1910 entrenching tool or "e-tool." Marines soon learned it was *never* called a "shovel." From late 1943 a folding e-tool began to be issued.

Marines in the frontline seldom attempted to shave, but when pulled out of the line, or the combat zone was secured, they reverted to normal grooming. The steel helmet universally served as a wash basin.

The jungle first aid kit was issued after 1943 in an effort to provide individuals with first aid and preventive medicine items necessary in the tropics. The poncho and shelter-half were olive-drab, but in 1943 reversible camouflage versions began to be issued.

Alternative web gear items were provided to accommodate weapons other than rifles. Automatic riflemen carried an M1936 six-pocket belt with each pocket holding two BAR magazines. Individuals armed with pistols, carbines, and submachine guns used a pistol belt with special pouches: a two-pocket pistol magazine pouch, two to four two-pocket carbine pouches, or three- or five-pocket submachine gun magazine pouches.

Weapons
The Marine Corps, first and foremost an infantry force, considered its most important weapons to be those arming its infantrymen: rifle, bayonet, automatic rifle, machine gun, carbine, rifle grenade launcher, and hand grenade. Other

weapons were also available to the infantryman: bazookas, flamethrowers, and demolition charges.

The rifle was the marine's basic arm. While country boys tended to have some experience with firearms, it was by no means near the level of skill required by the Corps. Most city boys had little if any firearms experience. A fair percentage of those familiar with firearms, though, had some degree of experience with bolt-action deer rifles, and they found the "03 Springfield" easy to operate.

The .30-cal. M1903 Springfield rifle had been in use by the Corps since 1908, providing legendary service. The old hands held it in reverence and recruits were expected to likewise regard it highly and learn everything there was to know about it. It was relatively light and compact at 8lb 11oz (3.95kg) and was 43¼in. (110cm) long, with a five-round magazine loaded by stripper clip. A slightly improved version, the M1903A1, was put into production in 1939, and in 1942 the M1903A3 was standardized to speed up production. While better finished and more refined than the Japanese Arisaka rifle, the two weapons were not dissimilar in capabilities. The Japanese 6.5mm round had less penetration and knockdown power, but their 7.7mm was about equal to the US .30-cal. Their rifles, though, were longer, and in the hands of smaller troops were a bit more awkward to handle in the jungle.

The Springfield armed the Corps through Guadalcanal. In early 1943 the semi-automatic .30-cal. M1 Garand rifle began to replace the "03." By late 1943 the FMF was completely armed with the M1. To the old timers the introduction of the M1 foretold the doom of the legendary Marine Corps marksmanship. They decried the M1 as too heavy and bulky at 9½lb (4.32kg; it was only a half-inch longer than the M1903), for being inaccurate, and too complex for dumb recruits to understand. The M1, however, proved to be a highly effective weapon, being fast to reload with an eight-round *en bloc* clip, and pumping out a higher rate of fire than an enemy armed with a five-shot bolt-action rifle.

An M1-armed marine could snap off 15–18 aimed shots in one minute, compared to an Arisaka-armed Japanese soldier's eight to ten rounds. While a bit heavier than he would have liked, most marines thought very highly of the M1, deeming it rugged and reliable, and they took extremely good care of it, as their lives and the lives of their buddies depended on its functioning.

With the rifle came a more basic weapon, the bayonet. The Japanese possessed a well-earned reputation for bayonet fighting, which they practiced for long hours, and the Marines were determined not to be outmatched. The 16-in. (40cm) bladed M1905 and M1942 bayonets were used on both the M1903 and M1. The 10-in. (25.4cm) M1905E1 and M1 bayonets began to be issued in 1943 to make them more usable at close-quarters. The Japanese had a 15½-in. (39.4cm) bayonet and a longer rifle, but their small stature limited their reach somewhat, and this was additionally countered by the typical marine's longer reach. The M1 carbine was not provided with its M4 bayonet until almost the war's end.

Springfields remained in use into 1944, as M7 rifle grenade launchers were not initially available for the M1 rifle, and stayed in use with ships' detachments, Marine barracks guards, and training and service units for some time. Rifle squads retained an M1903 with an M1 grenade launcher. The launchers gave the squad the ability to project grenades farther than hand-thrown grenades. Grenade types included M9A1 antitank, M17 fragmentation, M19 white phosphorus, and colored smoke and signal flares. Fragmentation hand grenades could also be fitted to a tailboom adapter and fired by grenade launchers. The M8 launcher was provided for the M1 carbine in 1944.

A weapon actually seeing wider use than the M1 rifle was the .30-cal. M1 carbine. A Marine division in 1943 had 8,000 rifles, but over 11,000 carbines. Officers, weapons crewmen, artillerymen, and most service and support personnel were armed with this light, compact weapon – a better alternative to the pistol. In fact, from April 1943 pistols were no longer issued to infantry and artillery regiments, being completely replaced by carbines. The semi-automatic carbine was fed by a 15-round detachable magazine. (The semi- and full-auto M2 with a 30-round magazine did not see combat in World War II.) The "baby Garand" was initially popular and much sought after by marines. It was light, compact, had a high-capacity magazine, and also looked slick. Once used in combat it was found wanting: while reliable enough it lacked range, penetration, and knockdown. It used a smaller .30-cal. cartridge than the M1 rifle – BAR, and Browning machine gun, little more than a pistol round. Another problem was that it sounded like a Japanese 6.5mm rifle. From early 1944 the squad's three assistant automatic riflemen were armed with carbines, but these weapons were soon replaced by M1 rifles. Squad and platoon leaders were armed with carbines, but many units replaced these too with rifles or submachine guns. While both the rifle and the carbine were designated M1, marines called the rifle simply the "M1" and the carbine just the "carbine."

Automatic riflemen were trained separately from riflemen, although the latter were familiar with and could operate an M1918A2 BAR. Here an instructor provides advice on the intricacies of stripping this complex weapon.

Thompson submachine guns were not common in rifle platoons: in 1943 a division had a pool of 78. The Thompson had long been in use by the Corps, who had found it useful in the Banana Wars, but it was little used in the Pacific. Three versions of the .45-cal. "Tommy gun" were employed by the Corps, the M1928A1, M1, and M1A1. They used 20- and 30-round magazines and were heavy, almost 11lb (5kg), and complex to disassemble and assemble. Its penetration through bamboo and brush was limited and it unfortunately also sounded like a Japanese 6.5mm machine gun.

The .30-cal. M1918A2 Browning Automatic Rifle was the second most important weapon in the squad. Two were assigned, and, from early 1944, three. It was heavy at 19lb 6oz (8.9kg), and bulky at 4ft (1.22m) in length. The flash suppressor was often removed to reduce its length by 3in. (7.6cm), and detaching the bipod knocked off 2½lb (1.14kg). Its 20-round magazines were heavy and deemed too small for sustained fire. It was accurate, though, and offered two rates of fire: the high 500–650rpm rate and the low 300–450rpm, which allowed single shots to be squeezed off. Yet it was complex and difficult to maintain. Marines were thankful that regulations prohibited white-glove inspections and timed disassembly and assembly. It was too easy to lose and damage the many small parts.

The hand grenade was another essential weapon. Grenades included the Mk II and Mk IIA1 "pineapple" fragmentation, Mk IIIA1 offensive "concussion" (½lb/0.23kg TNT) for blasting pillboxes, AN-M8 white smoke for screening, AN-M14 thermite incendiary for destroying enemy equipment, M15 white phosphorus (WP), and Mk 1 illuminating

An M1 carbine-armed marine demonstrates the kneeling throwing position with the Mk II "pineapple" fragmentation hand grenade. Grenades proved to be a key weapon on the Pacific islands.

burning for 25 seconds at 55,000 candlepower to illuminate a 100-yard (90m) radius area. The WP was especially useful for knocking out pillboxes and attacking troops in uncovered positions. Burning WP particles showering into positions stuck to whatever they came in contact with. Panicked soldiers hit by WP might try to wipe the sticky substance off, burning at 5,000°F (2,760°C), only to smear it over a wider area as it burned through them. M16 and M18 colored smoke grenades were used to mark positions and provide simple signals. The M16 came in red, yellow, green, violet, orange, blue, and black. The M18 generated a more vivid smoke cloud more rapidly and was issued in only the first four colors. Colored smoke rifle grenades, and hand grenades, fitted to rifle grenade adapter tailbooms, were used to mark targets for tanks. Marines would remove the fuse and scrape out half the smoke compound, as the full load obscured the target. A basic load of "frag" grenades was two per man, but it was common to carry a "double-dose," a double load. Grenades were used in such enormous numbers that during some island fighting their use rate far exceeded forecasts and an emergency resupply of grenades had to be flown in, sometimes depleting depot stockpiles. A common technique was to "cook-off" frags, that is, pull the arming pin, release the safety lever, count to two or three, and chuck it into a firing port. Because the grenade had a 4.5–5-second delay the enemy did not have time to recover it and toss it out.

Using demolitions was an important skill. Each platoon had a trained demolition corporal in anticipation for a raiding mission. Raiding was not to be an infantry role in the Pacific, but the emphasis on demolitions served the Corps well, owing to the enemy's extensive use of pillboxes and caves.[7] The two most common demolition items were the ½lb (0.23kg) TNT block, issued 100 in a wooden box, and the satchel charge. Multiple TNT blocks could be taped together, placed in sandbags or in other bags, or linked together with detonating cord, and detonated by a delay fuse ignited by a friction fuse lighter. Marines sometimes taped a TNT block to a "frag" grenade as a more potent pillbox popper. Satchel charges contained eight 2½lb (1.14kg) M2 tetrytol demolition blocks linked together by detonating cord at 8-in. (20cm) intervals as an M1 chain demolition charge. The 20lb (9kg) of explosives, slightly more powerful than TNT, were usually sufficient to destroy pillboxes. Another assault technique was to tape demolition charges to 81mm mortar shells and chuck them into caves.

Flamethrowers – "Zippos" or "Blowtorches" – did not see much use until the November 1943 Tarawa assault, but they proved invaluable for defeating pillboxes and caves. The M1A1 flamethrower was heavy – 70lb (32kg) with 4 gallons (15 liters) of thickened fuel. It was quite a load for a man to carry. An assistant operator would carry a 5-gallon (19-liter)

7 See Rottman, Gordon L., Osprey Fortress 1, *Japanese Pacific Island Defenses 1941–45*, Osprey, Oxford (2003).

refill fuel can and a spare compressed gas propellant tank. The range with thickened fuel was up to 50 yards (46m), but in practice it was shorter. In a continuous burst the flamethrower could burn for eight to ten seconds, but two-second bursts were normal. Rather than waste fuel by burning it as it was fired at targets, operators would sometimes "wet-down" the pillbox with a spray of un-ignited fuel and then WP grenades or Molotov cocktails were thrown. It is an understatement to say flamethrower operators led a dangerous and often short life. The Japanese would put the hated weapon under intense fire (detonation of the fuel tanks seldom occurred, that is a Hollywood invention). Heat exhaustion from bearing the load was common.

Quartermasters inspect KA-Bar fighting knives, virtually a symbol of the Corps. The man to the right is checking the edge of a hospital corps knife.

The 2.36-in. M1A1 antitank rocket launcher was another key weapon. The "bazooka" or "stovepipe" was introduced in time for Tarawa and for the first time infantrymen had a light, portable direct-fire weapon capable of knocking out a tank or pillbox with a shaped-charge warhead. It had a range of 250 yards (226m) although more practical ranges were 50–70 yards (46–64m).

Flamethrowers and bazookas did not have dedicated crewmen; instead specially trained riflemen were assigned. The two weapons were pooled at battalion level and there were sufficient numbers to provide one per squad, although the Marines did not always use this many. Two more weapons found at company level, however, were provided with dedicated crews. The .30-cal. M1919A4 Browning light machine gun was a tripod-mounted weapon, of which three were assigned to the weapons platoon. Normally one would be attached to each rifle platoon. There were also three 60mm M2 mortars, the company commander's "hip-pocket artillery." These operated as a section under central control and could deliver high-explosive and WP rounds out to 1,985 yards (1,814m).

There is one final weapon that was important to the infantryman, the KA-Bar fighting knife, virtually a symbol of the Corps. The Union Cutlery Company offered its heavy-duty fighting knife to the Corps in 1942. The Marines adopted it and other companies also manufactured

Pillbox assault training on Maui, Hawaii. Mock-up fortifications like this flamethrower-scorched concrete pillbox were constructed, with most concealed in vegetation.

it, but it became popularly know as the "KA-Bar." The name came from a customer's endorsement, a fur trapper who crudely wrote that his rifle had jammed and he used their knife to kill a wounded bear attacking him. In thanking the company the trapper described using the knife to "kill a bar." The way his writing was scrawled across the paper, it looked like "ka bar." The Quartermaster General advised against its adoption, claiming it was too expensive for the good it would do, and that too many marines would be injured by their own knives. Fortunately the Commandant ignored the recommendation.

BELIEF AND BELONGING

Faith in the Corps and loyalty to squad and platoon were the primary motivating factors for most marines. Some veterans compare their indoctrination and compulsory dedication to the Corps to brainwashing, but few bear any regrets. They understood the necessity for cohesion, and the sense of belonging this instilled. Marines did not fight for America, the flag, democracy, or their families: they fought for one another, for their comrades, and the Corps recognized this.

Their motivation against the Japanese was another thing. It was basic – veterans simply said the "Japs," or "Nips" as they called them, were doing a wrong that had to be righted. If the enemy wanted to die for their emperor, the marines would help them. The more the US troops heard about the Japanese, the more determined they were. Young marines liked to win, and they did not like to see buddies killed. By this time the stories of the Japanese being supermen had been dispelled. Nor did the stories of Japanese snipers, atrocities against Americans, and the fact that the Japanese never took prisoners, frighten them. The marines felt they were better trained and equipped, and that right was on their side.

It was the old hands, the old salts among the NCOs and the prewar Marine officers with long service in Latin America, China, and at sea with the fleet, who instilled the traditions of the service that were so important to making the new Corps what it was. Nonetheless, they endlessly bemoaned the demise of the "Old Corps" prior to the 1940 expansion.

There is no disputing that life in the Corps was rough and demanding. The Corps came first, over family and self. Only the barest concerns were paid to comfort and diversions. The hours were long, the work hard, and the discipline harder. They hated Army "dogfaces" only because they were told by their NCOs that they were worthless, that they lacked pride and tradition. They really had no idea about the Army, having never worked with soldiers and only having seen some on leave, mainly antiaircraft and coastal artillery troops while on liberty.

The marine's squad was his immediate family, a dozen men in whom he developed absolute trust. His platoon became an extended family under the guiding eye of its patriarch, the platoon commander, and even more so, the platoon sergeant, usually an old hand with prewar experience in exotic lands. The company commander, the "Skipper" or "Ol' Man" (usually in his mid-20s), oversaw his fiefdom aided by the 1st sergeant ("Top"). The marine was imbued with a sense of total loyalty to his unit and the Corps. There is an old saying, "Once a marine always a marine." There is more truth to this than mere hype.

B

Marksmanship training, Camp Elliott

The infantryman's weapons

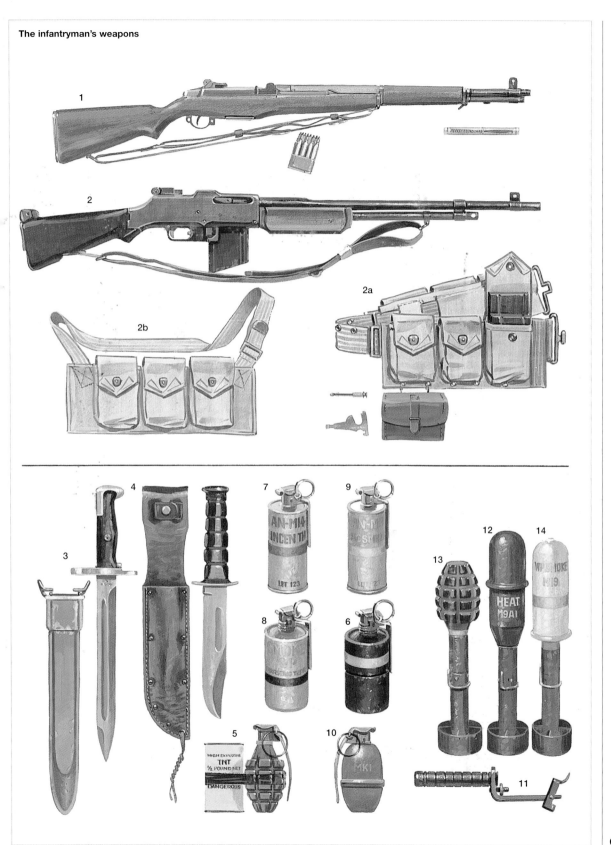

D

Namur blockhouse assault

"Duty beyond the sea"

F

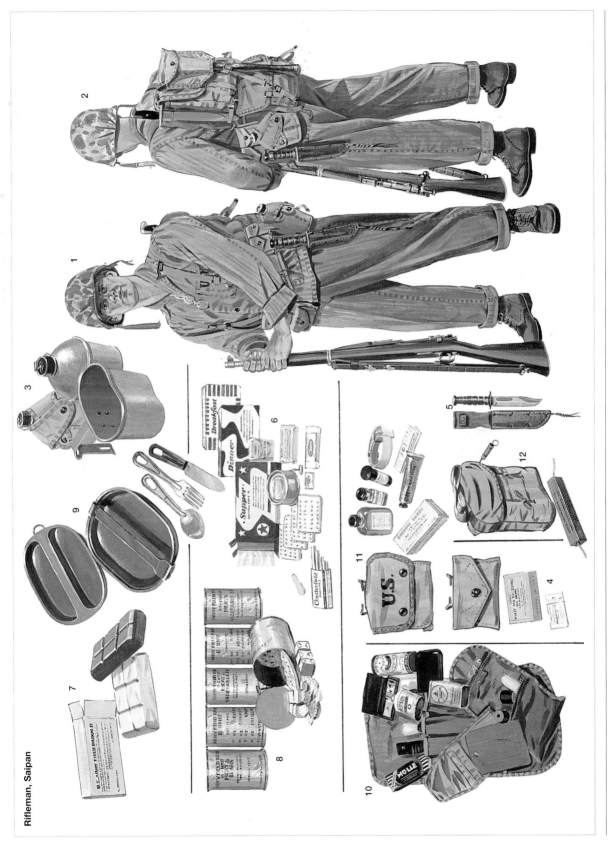

Saipan aid station